A DORLING KINDERSLEY BOOK

Senior Editor Jane Yorke
Editor Dawn Sirett
Senior Art Editor Mark Richards
Art Editor Jane Coney
Designer Margo Beamish-White
Production Marguerite Fenn

Photography by Philip Dowell
Additional Photography by Jerry Young (pages 6-7)
Illustrations by Martine Blaney, Dave Hopkins, and Colin Woolf
Animals supplied by Trevor Smith's Animal World

First published in Great Britain in 1991
by Dorling Kindersley Limited,
9 Henrietta Street, London WC2E 8PS

Text copyright and photography (pages 6-7)
copyright © 1991 Dorling Kindersley Limited, London
Photography (pages 4-5 and 8-21) copyright © 1991 Philip Dowell

A CIP catalogue record for this book is
available from the British Library.

ISBN 0-86318-460-X

Reproduced by Colourscan, Singapore
Printed and bound in Italy by L.E.G.O., Vicenza

·EYE·OPENERS·

Zoo Animals

DORLING KINDERSLEY • LONDON

Elephant

Elephants are very big animals. They have long noses called trunks. Elephants use their trunks to pull down leafy branches to eat. They also use them to squirt water into their mouths when they want a drink.

tusk

ear

trunk

tail

7

Camel

Camels live in hot, dry deserts. They carry people or heavy loads on long journeys. A camel can last for many days without food or a drink of water. It stores food in its hump.

eye

tail

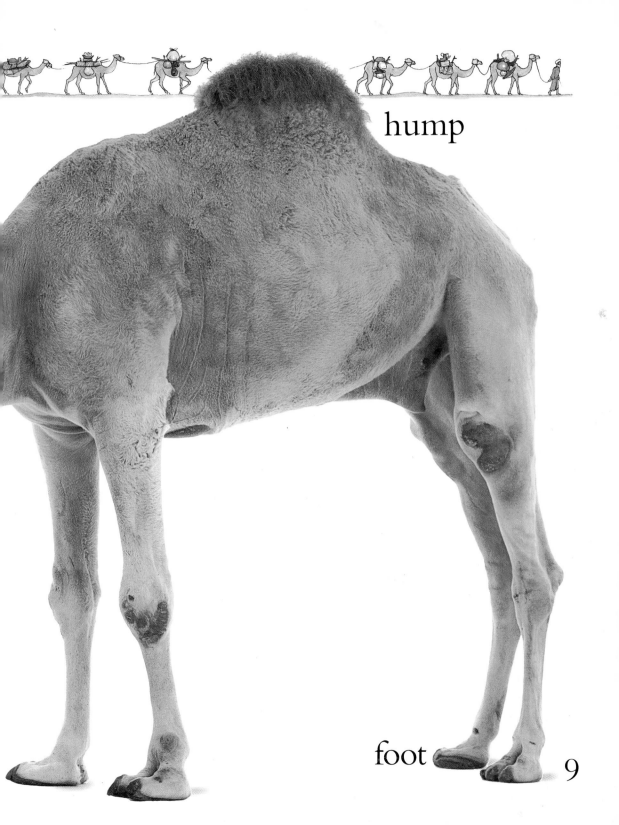

hump

foot

9

Monkey

Monkeys live high up in the
tree tops. They are good climbers.
They use their strong arms to swing quickly
from branch to branch. Monkeys eat fruits,
plants, birds' eggs, and insects. They spend
a lot of time grooming each other.

tail

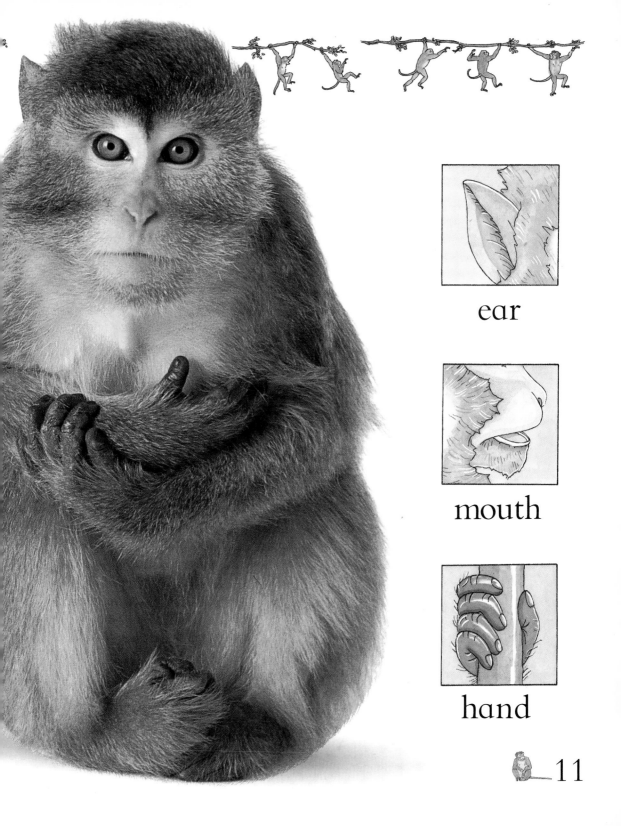

ear

mouth

hand

11

Zebra

Wild zebras live on hot, grassy plains. They have black-and-white striped coats. The stripes make them difficult to see in the long grass. This helps to keep them safe from fierce, hungry lions.

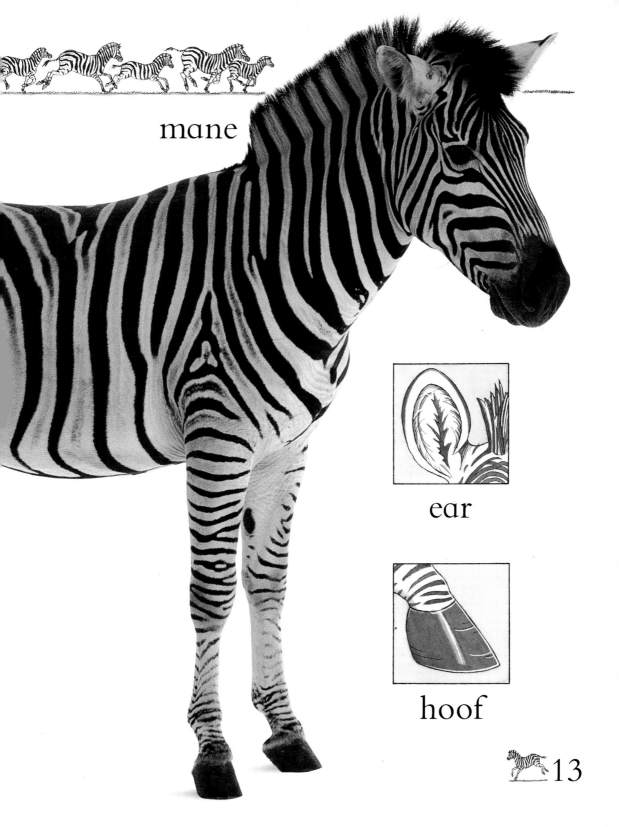

mane

ear

hoof

13

Parrot

Most parrots have bright, colourful feathers. They are noisy birds that usually live in trees. Parrots break open nuts and seeds with their sharp beaks.

14

wing

beak

feathers

tail

15

Tiger

tiger cub

This tiger cub will grow
into a fierce big cat.
Wild tigers spend their
days sleeping in
the long grass.
They hunt
at night.

paw

16

fangs

tail

17

Snake

A snake slithers along on its belly. Its body is covered in smooth scales. Most snakes live on the ground. They can climb trees by wrapping themselves around branches. Some snakes are also good swimmers.

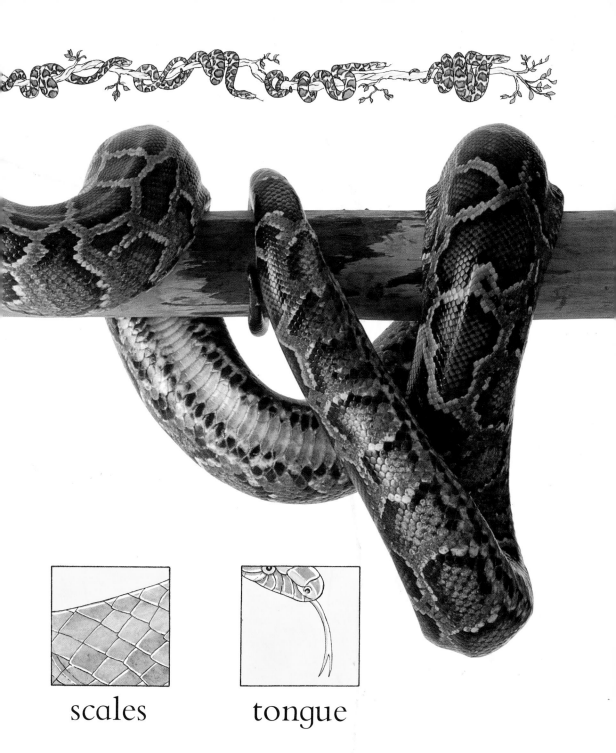

scales   tongue

19

Penguin

Wild penguins live in cold, icy countries. These birds cannot fly, but they can swim very fast. They move through the water using their short wings as paddles. Penguins dive into the sea to catch fish.

beak

foot

wing

21